Are You Addicted?

Stacy Hoare and Amy Muir

NWKBooks

Copyright: Stacy Hoare and Amy Muir. 2010

Stacy Hoare and Amy Muir hereby assert their rights to be identified as the owners of this work in accordance with section 77 to 78 of the Copyright Designs and Patents Act 1988.

All rights reserved. No part of this book may be reproduced in any form or by any electronic or mechanical means, including information storage or retrieval systems, without permission in writing from the publisher, except by a reviewer who may quote brief passages.

British Library Cataloguing Publication Data.
A catalogue record for this book is available from the British Library

Published by NWKBooks – www.nwkmedia.com

ISBN 978-1-907502-07-1

North West Kent College
Dartford
Kent

British Library Cataloguing Publication Data.
A catalogue record for this book is available from the British Library

The air outside was so fresh and cold that I couldn't wait to get into the warmth. Walking into the tiny, old-fashioned hall that was as dark as a cave and smelt like damp wasn't exactly the highlight of my day. The wallpaper was peeling off and the ceiling, which was obviously once white, was now a dirty egg shell colour. This wasn't exactly what I was expecting. I'd seen the advert whilst reading my favourite glossy magazine, I was expecting something different, very different. I expected a bit more class than this. I didn't even think that places like this still existed. I thought places like this had gone out when ankle swingers went out of fashion. I didn't want to be here, I really didn't, but I was doing this for me. Something needed to change and I was the only one who could take the first step.

They say that to be addicted to something you have to need it rather than want it. You know you are addicted to something when that something consumes your life every minute of everyday. You stop caring about everything around you except that one thing. You forget about your friends and family and the people around you, all you care is about that one thing, nothing else. Addiction is dangerous. This place wanted to help young people like myself with addictions. I knew I had to go.

Walking into the tiny hall, I saw about ten or so faces turn around and look. Many of them smiled at me. This was not what I had expected at all. I had never walked into a room and not felt judged. I've always been paranoid that people judge me and know about my dirty little secret - people on the street, people in the shops, people just going about their daily business. So the fact that everyone seemed so welcoming was nice. Different. Taking a seat at the end of the circle I felt relived, and kind of excited. Nobody in the room looked the same, everyone was different and unique, but nobody looked extremely ill or washed out. Just by looking at the faces I couldn't tell whose addiction was what, it wasn't apparent what was wrong with them.

I sat back in my chair and began to relax.

A small woman, maybe in her late fifties, introduced herself as Sue. She welcomed everyone, and asked a simple question, 'What does addiction mean to you?'

Everyone said their opinion, each one better the first, and then it was me. My mouth was dry and my palms were moist. I took a deep breath. I had never talked about this before, I took another breath and began to speak.

"To me addiction is something I can't control; it's a want and a need. Whenever I have money I get my fix. I've never stolen from my family, but I've been tempted. If I don't get what I need I fear I will go insane."

Sitting down I saw all the eyes on me. I was waiting for a rash comment or a snigger, but there was nothing, everyone smiled at me. I felt for the first time in my life, comfortable.

Leaflets were being handed out and with just a glimpse I saw something that made my heart stop. Something that made me lost for breath, it read: They say that admitting that you have a problem is the first step in battling your addiction; and I myself have realised how true this really is. I never had realised how easy it would be for someone to get hooked on something so simple. I used to come home every night and it would be there staring me dead in the eyes, it was so tempting and I knew it wouldn't take me long to give in. It gave me a rush, it made me feel needed and wanted; it was love.

I have never honestly read something that was connected to the way that I felt before, it was exactly how I was feeling. It was like all my thoughts were down on paper.

I guess I'd never been somewhere where I'd felt this accepted before. It felt different, but good. But the part that I was ever so nervous was about to start, the words "tell me about yourself" rung in my ears. I stood up and began to speak.

I began to speak softly.

"Hello, my name is Kate Ashdown and I am an alcoholic. Nobody has, and no-one ever will, realise how hard this was for me to admit. It's taken a long time for me to finally admit this, and standing here in front of all of you today shows me how much my hard work is paying off."

I saw the smiles from around the room and I grew more confident.

"If I had said to myself four years ago that I would be confident enough to tell you this I would have laughed. I was 19 when I first started drinking heavily. I kept it my dirty little secret. I was too ashamed. Now I am nearly there. I am nearly over my addiction to alcohol. Yes, a common addiction, but not something you'd like to be addicted to. Trust me. I never want to go back to how I was. Drinking was always an easy way for me to escape the real world. It was a world where nothing mattered, no one would criticise me for doing something silly, or acting different. Everyone understood. I say everyone - I mean myself and my mind. Having an addiction is like being in a special world though. There are no rules and you can do what you want, there's nobody there to tell you what your doing is wrong.

I was leading a normal life with a 9 to 5 job in an office. I studied Secretarial Skills at college and was lucky to even get a job. You hear of people all the time being depressed with no job so they turn to booze. So, I thought there was something seriously wrong with me to always rely on alcohol. What was wrong with me? I'd ask myself this regularly. Then it hit me. I would get in from work, switch on the TV and grab a bottle of wine. That bottle of wine would turn into 3 bottles of wine throughout the duration of the evening. That same routine would happen every weeknight. Taking that first sip after a busy day at work was like heaven to me, all my troubles melted away. But what troubles? I didn't have a father. But that was the past, why would it bother me now? I didn't talk to my mother but I didn't care for that. Or did I? I didn't have a boyfriend. I had myself and my flat mate. Then I realised. Was I drinking excessively to heal the pain of my father?

The moment I got the phone call I felt my world fall to pieces around me, and there was nothing I could do about it. I tried to stop it, but my world had crumbled right in front of my face. My father died when I was just 19 years old, it was the result of a car accident, he was hit off of his bike by a driver of a land rover. His head hit the ground and he was instantly killed. I had never been close to my father but this wasn't something that I wanted to experience. I wouldn't have wished this pain and hurt on anyone; nobody deserves to feel like that.

I started drinking more than usual. I drunk when I went out with my friends, and I'd get stupidly drunk. At the weekend, everyone would indulge. You'd go out on the streets to clubs and pubs and everyone would be in the same state. But I thought I was better then everyone else. I wouldn't join in with my friends when they decided to take drugs. I controlled myself, but when it came to alcohol I had no control. My boyfriend broke up with me soon after my father was killed. I'd been with him since I was 14 years old. Long time huh? He was the one who was there for me, he was the one who supported me, he was the one who made me better and helped me cope. He broke up with me for a good reason though. I don't blame him for doing so. I guess it was just all too much. I had the most terrible mood swings. I blame myself. It was all a downwards spiral from there, without him I was nothing. I thought that alcohol would take the pain away, help heal my broken heart, how silly I was to think this. But I hadn't lost all the men in my life; I found a new man, Jack. Jack didn't ask any questions, he never needed me, I would always need him. He was there when I went to work and there when I got home. He was there for the good days and the bad. He was what I thought was perfect, the perfect man. He was thin and black; he was hard to swallow but went down well. He was the resolution to all my pain and hurt, he was perfect. Just touching him with my tongue would make my whole body quiver with excitement; just one touch from him would make my body numb. He was a bottle of liquid perfection, liquid gold.

After a couple of years of finishing a bottle or two in the evening I slowly started cutting back. I thought to myself, I didn't need alcohol, it wasn't going to heal anything. But then one day I had a relapse. I can still remember that day. It was a cold winters evening, and it hit me like a ton of bricks to the face. It was a feeling I had never felt before, a feeling of emptiness and confusion. I didn't understand it, at first I was confused. But slowly it sunk in and I just knew what was happening. I never got hangovers, I didn't even really know what a hangover was. I always felt tired after a night of drinking but never did I ever feel as rough as I did that day. I felt weak and woozy, I tried to stand up but I felt my stomach drop. It was a weird feeling, a feeling I didn't want. I thought I just needed something to eat. So I tried to make some toast, but the strong smell of the bread burning made my stomach turn. I was going to be sick; I needed to be sick. I was sick. Pulling my head out of the sink was hard, I felt so weak, so unable to move. I was sick over ten

times. It was then that I realised I needed to sort myself out. At the age of 22, I wasn't getting any younger, and I was in serious need of sorting myself out.

So I came to the decision to stop drinking alcohol. I didn't know how I was going to go about it. I knew it wasn't something that would happen overnight. I knew I was about to head off into a rollercoaster of ups and downs but I knew I could do it. I was better than that. I cut down massively. I didn't need to drink whilst being alone. I socially had a glass or two, but I didn't end up chucking back as much as I used to. I occasionally had slip ups, everyone does, but slowly I was battling my addiction. This was 6 months ago. I've done so well, I know I have."

After I had finished talking, everyone clapped. Wow, I had never been applauded for telling people about who I really am. I was shocked. I didn't think that people would understand me. I thought I was alone. I've never in my life been applauded for being me, for telling the truth. All I'd ever got was sniggers and dirty looks, but not today. The room was filled with smiling faces. I felt at home. I felt acceptance from this small little hall filled with people that I had never met before in my life. For the first time in my life I was proud, proud to be me.

Next to speak was a boy who looked very young. It didn't seem right, him standing there with some type of addiction. He looked like he should have still been in secondary school. He was shy and found it hard to stand up in front of the rest of us. Sue said he could turn his back to the group if he wanted to whilst talking about his addiction. He agreed and turned around. He said his name was William Curtis, and that he was 18 years old.

"It is an addiction to need something, and I need to play games. I don't just want it. I need it. So yeah, you could say I'm addicted to games. Not only am I addicted to games, but fantasy too. It's not unusual. If you were to ask any girl what her boyfriend or boy friends love to do, she'd most probably say playing games. My friends and family always tease me, telling me I have no life and should have better things to do. That's easy for them to say. I admit that I do tend to isolate myself from any kind of social contact. But what's wrong with that? I'd rather stay indoors than go out. That's my own choice. I mean, yeah, I always mean to do other normal things, such as tidying my room, doing my college work, or spending time with my little brothers and sisters, but I can't because gaming interferes and takes all of my attention. All of my focus is entirely on game achievements. I couldn't care less for real life events.

I've played games on game consoles since the age of 5. Obviously as I got older, I became aware of the internet and its fantastic uses. My addiction to playing games got worse. I needed to play some sort of game everyday. I wouldn't be able to get through a day knowing that I couldn't play a game. Playing these games help my daily stresses go away. Games to me are like cigarettes to a chain smoker. Someone will smoke if they're bored or stressed. I will play a game. However, I've started smoking in between raiding and dungeons to relax and reduce nerves. Even though this is a bad thing, it really helps me relax. Games have made my health deteriorate badly. I've become addicted to energy drinks and caffeine tablets so I can stay awake for days on end to maximise game play.

I play games because it gets me away from everything, cheers me up and makes the bad things go away. When I'm angry or upset I'll go and play a game. Anything violent, anything with aggression and a sadistic storyline. People take drugs or get drunk to make themselves feel happier. I do the same with games. It's the sort of freedom to do anything. To immerse myself in fantasy where things I'd like to be real are real in the gaming world. I get to pretend I'm of the Emperor's Space Marines, genetically and psycho-doctrined super human soldiers that defend the human race across galaxies and star systems in 41st millennium. Fantasy worlds like Warhammer 40k to me are just so much cooler and more appealing than real life. Life is boring; there's no magic, no demons, no monsters, no vampires or lycans. Fantasy worlds are so much more appealing. I like to immerse myself in them and pretend I'm there, and escape the dull pretences of the real world. Yeah, OK, so you probably couldn't care less or even understand all this gaming talk. But I just want you all to understand that being addicted to games is like being addicted to cocaine. I need my fix. It may seem weird to you lot and other people, but no-one understands except for me. It's just that fantasy worlds with magic and demons are so much more intriguing. They aren't ruled by the laws of physics and simple human minds. I like the idea of living in the fantasy world rather than the world we live in now.

There's a pretty harmless release when compared to drugs and alcohol etc. However, I know full well that games can lead people to doing dangerous things. It can have a massively dangerous affect on teenagers especially. I've heard stories of teenagers killing people just like how

they kill people in games. I like the violence and wars in the games. I like killing people, causing destruction and inflicting pain on others in the games. I often think about how people have hurt me and how badly I want to hurt them back in real life, so violent games with blood, gore and killing are an easy way of, I guess, "acting" that out. I don't want to sound psycho, I'm just trying to be as honest as possible. I get to pretend my victim in the cyber world is the person I hate in the real world. I get to hurt them, make them bleed. I like the sense of getting to do things in games that I couldn't do to the people I hate in real life, without being arrested or such. Don't get me wrong, I wouldn't be able to hurt a fly in real life, and this is why games are good for me."

After he had stopped speaking, a woman who introduced herself as Lauren Gold stood up. She then began to speak about her own addiction to smoking. She didn't muck about. I could just tell that she was one of them girls that could talk for Britain.

"It didn't take me long to get hooked, it was easy. It helped me when I was stressed and when boredom struck. It cured my hunger and helped me socialise. It was more than an addiction to me, it was a want, a need. I didn't mean to start; it was just a bit of harmless fun. When someone brought some fags into school I thought it would just be something to try. I tried it once, and tried it again. I didn't like the taste; I just liked how it went down oh so easily. I felt grown up and I was only young. It made me feel older and I thought I looked cool. I loved the disapproving looks old people gave me, it made me feel powerful.

I used to hide it from my mum so well, she had never smoked and she was very anti-smoking, but the smell was easy to hide. All that was needed was a bit of perfume, just something to cover the smell. Even when she told me my teeth were starting to turn yellow, she never clocked. I remember having a boyfriend in school, but he dumped me for reeking of smoke all the time. If it was up to me I probably would have stopped smoking but so many of my friends encouraged me. I would never buy fags for myself. I always used to ponse off of my friends, people off of the street - people rarely said no. All I had to do was flash abit of chest and they were putty in my hand. Boys my age loved me; I was nice, too nice. They would go to the shop and buy me some fags if they "thought" that they were going to get something. They wanted me, and I knew it. I always thought that was a bad way for a 14 year old to act, but whatever, I got what I wanted. And from there I've never looked back.

As I got older, I said I would quit but I never did. At a party I couldn't resist having one, it went down so well with a glass of wine, helped me socialise and meet new people. OK, it's not a good way to meet people, but I thought it was a good way to start a conversation in the pub garden. I would go outside for the fresh air, but then someone would offer me a fag and I couldn't say no. Every time I tried to quit I just felt like it was pulling me back in, someone would offer me one, and BAM! That one would turn to lots more. At work smoking would help me on a bad day to calm down and relax; never did I think that it would affect my health that bad. I mean when you're having a stressful day, a fag and a coffee is perfect. I know, nicotine and caffeine, my diet was a walking killer but it got me through the day.

They say that when you smoke for a long period of time your body changes - your teeth go yellow and your complexion ends up looking bad. But I didn't care about that, none of that had bothered me. The only thing I was worried about was quitting. Everyone knows when you quit you put on a stone that you will never lose, so I guess I was smoking to keep my size 10 figure.

I never knew smoking could affect you that bad though. I knew it could give you lung cancer, but you always think "that will never happen to me".

And you always see the quit smoking adverts on the TV and radio. They talk about dying and illnesses but you never think twice that it would happen to you. How wrong I was. I used to get chest pains all the time, but I thought that was because I wasn't very fit. I never exercised so I thought that was to blame. I complained about it to my sister, and she told me I should go get it checked out. I was only young though; it couldn't possibly have been that bad, could it?

It was a Tuesday afternoon

in April when I found out the extent of my smoking. I only went to the doctors for a quick check-up to make my sister happy. All I thought they would say was I needed to cut down on the smoking and give me a slap on the wrist, that's what they always did, but today something seemed different.

Instead of just walking in and out, they did some tests on me, blood samples, and all sorts. I felt confused as I waited in the waiting room. "Fifteen minutes till you get your results" they told me, but an hour and half later I was still waiting. I knew something was wrong; they wouldn't have kept me here for no reason. Then the doctor called me into his office.

He asked me to sit down and brace myself, but for what I was about to hear I couldn't have prepared myself enough. I didn't believe it at first, I knew I was in pain but I never thought that something I loved so much could do this to me. I mean, how could something so simple harm me so much? Smoking was almost the killer of me. I was diagnosed with a collapsed lung. I thought my shortness of breath was just because of my weight gain. I didn't realise I had harmed myself so much.

He said to me that I had to choose, quitting or death... and for the first time in my life I knew the answer. I guess that's what changed it for me; the medication I was on was a killer. It reduced my craving for smoking, and slowly I reduced the amount of nicotine in my body. It took a collapsed lung for me to change my lifestyle around, something that I shouldn't have started in the first place, and something that I shouldn't have continued. I guess I should regret starting in the first place but I don't.

It's something that has affected me greatly and a great story to tell my children when I finally have some, because before I decided to quit, the dream of having kids was just that, a dream. A dream that was nearly taken away from me.

Thank you very much."

Wow. Hearing her story left me speechless and as I looked around the room, I saw some faces similar to mine. It took someone close to death to actually realise what they were doing was wrong. This woman was a role model. She didn't feel sorry for herself at all, she knew what she had done was her own fault. She said that she was going to go to start going into primary and secondary schools to teach kids about the effects of smoking. Everyone clapped her and told her that she was an inspiration.

Next, a boy of 18 stood up and introduced himself. He said his name was Ben Carpenter. He then went around and shook everyone's hand. He seemed like the typical charmer with his cheeky personality and blonde curls. It was no surprise when he said his addiction was sex.

"So I'm addicted to sex. Not only do I want it all the time, I need it. I have no problem with admitting that I am obsessed with sex. Not just sex, but the whole sex package, including porn and foreplay. As long as it involves genitals I'm there. C'mon, don't look at me like that. It's not my fault I'm surrounded by beautiful women is it?

I lost my virginity at the age of 15, a pretty decent age if you ask me. Ever since then I've had about 40 sex partners and no, I wasn't in a relationship with any of them. Yes I know, I'm only 18 and I've had 40 sex partners. Shock horror. But let me tell you something. I always use protection and I never lead a girl on. I always let a girl know that it's just sex and nothing more. It takes two to tango. That's all I'm saying.

If I could I'd have sex numerous times a day, and depending on how hungry I got, that would determine how many times I'd stop for a break. If I'm not having sex, I'm thinking about it or trying to subtly seduce girls. Usually my charm always works, but I have been told to "get lost" quite a few times. That's fair enough, I'm not for everyone. My charm works better over the internet. My most affective line on MSN is "so you gonna bang me or what?" I'm not being rude, I just know that girls like it when boys are forward and a bit cheeky, right? It's all a bit of harmless fun anyway!

My sex addiction is like a form of OCD – sexual compulsivity. I came across a statement on the internet that describes me perfectly. "Sex addicts spend whole days consumed by sexual thoughts. They develop elaborate fantasies, find new ways of obtaining sex and mentally revisit past experiences, because their minds are so preoccupied by these thoughts." That statement was made for me. Also on the internet, I found people saying that sex addictions were like drug and drink addictions. Well I don't believe that sex addictions are like drug and drink addictions because a sex addiction cannot drive you to stronger sex. Drug addictions drive you to stronger drugs and so on, but no matter how much sex I have, I would never move onto rape or paedophilia.

There's nothing wrong with sex anyway and if you think there is, then there's something wrong with you! It's perfectly normal. Sex is good. If I want it, and she wants it, then hurray! Without sex I feel like I'm going to explode. I mean, porn is good for a while when lonely, as is my right hand, but there comes a point when you become desperate and need the real thing.

I hate it when my friends mention the opposite sex or mention the fact that they've got laid recently even if they are in a relationship. I don't do relationships myself. I am happier single than in a relationship because I have more choice. Like the world, vagina must be explored vastly and you can only do that through travel. I want to travel and I'm not basing it around sex, I'm basing it on vagina. There's a rumour that if you bang enough global vagina, you can actually have sex everyday of your life when you return. Wishful thinking? Maybe.

When I get sex it's amazing, like I'm in heaven, and it's never stopped any ambitions but sometimes I've not done things like homework in order to go get some sex. Rebel, I know."

After he had finished everyone giggled. He was most definitely a cheeky chap.

Next was a young woman who was absolutely stunning. I couldn't think of why she'd be here; everything about her seemed perfect. Maybe she had come to the wrong place. Someone should tell her that she wasn't attending an interview to become a top model and that this was a place for addictions. Then she spoke. She said her name was Lola Rose and that she was addicted to looking good. Typical, I thought.

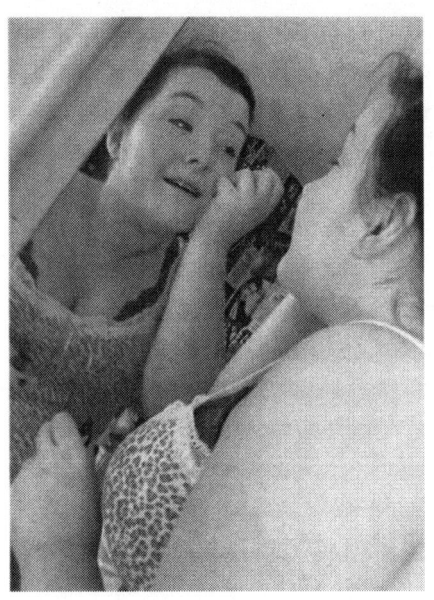

"They say the first step to fixing a problem is admitting you have one. Done. I have an addiction to looking good. They also say the first sign of having a problem is denial. Been there, done that. I won't deny it anymore. I didn't think that wanting to look your best all the time was a problem. Now I do. Its hard work you know, wanting to look your best all the time. It becomes too much at times but I'd rather look my best than my worst. If you never look your best, then people will expect the worst of you and I want people to expect the best.

Make-up, fake tan and hair extensions will never hurt a girl or anyone else for that matter. It's my choice what I want to do with my hair, face and body. My hair and make-up must always be picture perfect. As well as wearing the best clothes that I can afford. Without all of this, I feel absolutely disgusting and ugly. When I feel like that I make sure no-one can see me. I don't go out until I know that I look good. It takes me ages to get ready, especially for a night out, because I'm so busy trying to look good. I always have to make sure I do everything perfectly and carefully, if I don't, I have to scrub it all off then start again. When I'm just going out, say to the shops or to a friend's house, I still spend a lot of time getting everything just perfect. I never just get up in the morning and do a slow morning routine; it's always shower, moisturise, fake tan, get dressed, do make-up, and then sort out hair. This can take me up to 2 - 3 hours everyday. I would NEVER be caught dead outside the house without so much as speck of make-up on my face, I feel so wrong without it.

If you were looking at my daily routine, your first thought would probably be "look how vain she is" or something like "she doesn't need all that make up". Thing is though, 1) I'm not actually vain at all. I'm very self-conscious. I'm always being called vain as I'm constantly looking in mirrors; reapplying my make-up every hour and I also take pictures of myself often. It's just a cover up of the fear I have that people will think bad of me if I don't look good. 2) I do need all this make up because it makes me look and feel better. That's all that matters right? That's the thing; why look rough when you can look so much better. I don't understand. I just hate looking rough. When I feel that I don't look good, I feel terrible and that everyone is judging me. If I see a girl who I think is prettier than me, I just want the ground to swallow me up. I hate the competition between girls. I always think people are talking about me and I always feel very paranoid. When I look good, I feel happy and I enjoy what I'm doing, from knowing I'm looking good. I feel people are looking at me in a good way and I enjoy the attention. It makes me feel better.

If my boyfriend compliments a girl about the way she looks or looks at another girl in a sexual manner, I feel sick and my tummy flips. I think that they don't think I'm good enough and it makes me want to look better than everyone else so their attention is only on me. I always look nice all the time and I make sure I'm 'perfect' when I see my boyfriend. I act desirable and confident so they don't see anyone else, so they are only attracted to me. I just make them more attracted to me so that I feel more secure as I'm very insecure inside. If someone made a bad comment about the way I looked, my self esteem would drop in an instant, even if it was a joke. I believe that I have to look good to get any of my wishes met. I love it when people compliment me. I love getting attention from people I don't know. I like knowing that people think I'm attractive. It's like I need the attention.

I would never consider plastic surgery in order to maintain looking good. I know I'd feel so much better in my natural body, even though I put make-up on and wear hair extensions. I want people to like me without plastic surgery. I don't have piercings anymore because I just prefer people to compliment my face, not unnatural things."

Looking up I saw a boy, he was tall with scruffy looking hair and a lot of stubble, and he looked like he hadn't left his room in days. He said his name was Kane and he lived just down the road. I'd never seen him before, but to be honest I would never have given him a second look; he looked like he needed a good wash. Then he spoke.

"I have an addiction to finding my other half. An addiction is a yearning lust of need from a desired substance or object - physical or metaphorical. Once you sampled something addictive, you will always need more. I suppose I have an addiction, an unreasoned desire for more, but it's more a craving than an addiction due to having felt such a force very rarely.

Through sorrow and madness, this craving formed, devoid of all knowledge, emotion and awareness, it desired to fill this hole, this craving was a craving unlike any other. My heart scarred and ripped apart but is now repaired, albeit with a rough hand. It craves to feel the warmth it lost and it feels that the warmth can only be found inside it's other half, its soul mate. It pines with sorrow, it whines with tears, it howls in agony, it screams in pain, it cries in vain, it roars with rage and love. A rage and love that knows no bounds, it would unleash all known forms of hell just to feel this closeness of its lover.

My physical self goes about my daily routines, talking with friends, completing college work, hanging out, sleeping, but behind this masked facade lies the cursed hope of completion. Everyday, my eyes are constantly watching, feeling, sampling the atmosphere, waiting, craving for a sign that I may have found the one I'm searching for, but this task is a burden; when your eyes only see what they want to see, how can you tell what's truth or lie?

I wait as long as time will stand; spreading my emotion like an aura as if to identify the one that matches my heart but as with every second of every minute of every day, my heart's aching persists with the force of a typhoon, knowing I haven't found them yet. When your emotions and your heart drive you as strongly as mine, it shows just how much you miss, yet how much you see.

To have ambition is to have a drive toward something, be it a job promotion, a life-long wish or even just to achieve a small time task. The knowledge of what drives you to achieve a goal is your ambition. In the general sense, what everyone calls ambition, I just call simple desire. To have ambition(s), is to aim high, to better yourself, to achieve something that you've never done before. It said that a person's life without purpose has no reason to live, but what of those who have lost their purpose, the ones beaten and broken by their peers and the world. Surely thoughts are spared for them? Alas, it's not the case for ones such as these people, myself included, so what is there to do when you lose the one thing that makes life worth living, your life's one main ambition? A destiny of sorts. Simple, you make a purpose of your own.

There's no use sitting around waiting for it to come slap you round the face, you make your purpose, your own reason to live, your own ambition, your own... destiny. While I feel the emptiness my heart wishes to fill, I also feel the drive, this urge, to fill this emptiness which can only be described as completion. With completion, only true happiness can be granted and once more you'll feel the force of your

emotion rising as you've completed your greatest journey to fulfill your ambition. This completion will (I hope) grant me eternal lease from a burden that cannot be shared. With my soul mate found, they'd be my heart and soul, the simplest gestures between us only glimpsing the emotion that exists between us, however... first I must find them, and even before that I must suffer this eternal rage, frustration and sadness when I see other couples, showboating their affections when not even they could understand this turmoil..."

Everyone was gob smacked. He looked like he belonged on the streets. I was in shock with the way he spoke; he spoke with such emotion and intelligence. I tried to put myself into his shoes, as being addicted to finding your other half just didn't seem right. By putting myself into his shoes I began to somehow feel the hole in his heart that needed completing. I related it to the way a hole was made into my heart when my dad was killed.

Next was a young woman who looked worse for wear. She had very heavy bags underneath her eyes. She seemed awkward, and nervous, like she didn't want to be there. She was obviously finding it hard to get words out of her mouth. She said her name was Christina Gallows. She then stared at us all for about a minute before turning around and walking out. Sue followed her as we all sat there unaware of what was going on. 5 minutes later, they were back. Christina said that she was sorry but she wasn't used to talking in front of large groups of people. She also said that she came back because she was doing it for her mum. She said she knew her mum would be so proud of her. That warmed my heart.

"Forget cannabis, forget heroin. I have an addiction to a different sort of drug. 'Everyday painkillers'. People ask how the hell you can become addicted to painkillers, because they taste like nothing. It's not what the pill tastes like that addicts you, it's what it does in your brain that addicts you. Part of the danger of painkillers is that people think because they are legal drugs they must be safe to use. They are also easy to get, since many families have painkillers in their medicine cabinets and they can be easily purchased in a shop.

Painkillers make me feel good and they're the only things that can get me through a day. Until now. I don't even know how I became addicted in the first place, it just kind of happened. I started getting unbearable aching pains in my back. I was constantly going back and forth from the doctors complaining. He put me on painkillers. They were wonderful. Finally I managed to sort out my back problems. However, I then started relying on painkillers whenever I felt unwell, or had a pain or ache. I kept getting headaches and painkillers just seemed to do the trick. I also found it difficult to sleep so I took a couple of painkillers before sleeping, just to help. It helped a lot.

I took a packet of painkillers with me wherever I went. I would go to the pub with my friends, come home, and take a couple and go to sleep. I'd then wake up with a hangover and take some more. I didn't really think of the tablets as medicine, I thought of them more as sweets. I took them when I felt angry, stressed or upset. They were like a chill pill too. Mum started to worry for me, as she knew I was taking them a lot, she thought something more serious was up with me. She tried making me go to the doctors but I didn't believe that I had a problem. She even stopped buying them, so I started buying them myself. I just couldn't go without, I needed them.

This was when I realised that I had an addiction to painkillers. Painkillers do not cure illness, the simply relieve symptoms, yet I took them as if they would cure my illness. I even took them once my so called symptoms cleared up. My body became addicted to them. My body developed a tolerance to the drugs.

So I'd take at least 6 - 8 tablets a day. I managed to stop taking them for up to a week but found myself back on them. I kept telling myself that I would stop but it just didn't happen. Until now. I haven't taken a pain killer in twenty days and counting. So yeah, it might not seem like a long time, but it is to me. I'm trying my best.

I decided to contact my local hospital to get help. I didn't go alone, my mum took me. She was right. I should have gone a long time ago. I'm now under treatment and being monitored very closely. Just because I haven't taken a painkiller for twenty days, doesn't mean that I haven't wanted to. I get the biggest and worst headaches. My instant reaction is to head over to the medicine cupboard. But all medicine has been taken out of my house now. My mum keeps a close eye on me.

I know that one day I'll be able to stop relying on painkillers. I've been told what I need to do and I'm going to do it. You don't recover from an addiction by just stopping. You recover by creating a new life where it is easier to not use. If you don't create a new life, then all the factors that brought you to your addiction will eventually catch up with you again."

When she finished talking, the statement kept rolling around in my head. It was true.

Next a young woman stood up and said her name was Natalie Watson. Straight away I knew what she was addicted to; she had 3 shopping bags next to her feet. No, she hadn't just popped into the supermarket before coming here, she had shopping bags with designer brands on.

"I have an addiction to shopping. When I feel lonely, I go shopping. When I feel angry, I go shopping. When I feel stressed, I go shopping. Shopping makes me feel better about everything. The only thing that annoys me about shopping and buying so many things is how fast my bank balance drops. Because of that I got myself a credit card. Yeah, it was probably not the best of ideas, but it needed to be done. If I'm not shopping, I'm thinking about it and if I'm not thinking about it, I'm talking about it.

I go shopping everyday without fail. I wake up in the morning and instantly have the urge to go shopping. I don't feel happy until I've actually done some shopping. I just feel depressed until then. Before I had a credit card, I'd see stuff in shops that I wanted to buy, but just couldn't afford. I'd starve myself and work overtime just so I could afford it next time. I actually feel like I need to go shopping in order to live. I believe that I wouldn't have the friends I have now, a job or a nice life, without the nice clothes and other nice things I've brought. I know that shopping and buying new stuff will help me succeed in life.

Not only do I have this terrible addiction to shopping, I have an addiction to designer brands. You think I'm joking? If you look into my wardrobe, you'll find nothing from Primark or any other non-designer brands. You'll find that everything is from all the shops celebrities and rich people would shop in. Ever since I was a little girl, I've always been wearing expensive clothes. My mum would dress me all up in the best gear. You wouldn't see me dead in cheap clothes. Some people say it doesn't matter. It does matter. Wearing clothes with a label makes me feel important. It makes me feel better than everyone else. I'll walk onto the street knowing that I've spent lots of money to feel and look this good. I know I'm coming across as rude and you could confuse it with ignorance. I'm not ignorant. I'm a very lovely girl. I accept everyone for who they are, but I'm allowed to be who I am too. This is who I am. I work in a clothes shop, which probably doesn't help my addiction to buying clothes as I'm always surrounded. I believe that you have to look good as what you wear and how you wear it says it all. If someone said I looked like a tramp or called me ugly, my self esteem would drop. No-ones ever been so nasty but the thought of it really upsets me. I definitely care about what others think of me.

Also, I would consider plastic surgery in order to look good in the near future. I would get my boobs, lips, and nose, under eyes, bum, thighs and more done if I needed it. I base looking good around my ambitions like getting a boyfriend and a better job in the future. I don't have a boyfriend at the moment but I've gone through a few. They complimented me all the time about how well I looked after myself."

Next was a girl who claimed that she had the same addiction as Natalie Watson. She said her name was Stacy Long and that she had an addiction to shopping too. Well, it's a common addiction I guess.

!Well I'm addicted to shopping too. Not because I want to look good and not because I'm materialistic either. I'm just far too attached to my possessions big or small. How can I break my addiction to stuff? You tell me. I have too much stuff, and I'm always buying more. A lot of it is stuff I don't really need - clothes and accessories I rarely wear, perfume and make-up in quantities beyond what I can reasonably use. I'm also addicted to keeping little things that mean something to me. I'll keep anything that will remind me of a certain day I've had.

I'm both a shopaholic and a packrat. I can never pare my belongings down to just the essentials, and I inevitably accumulate more than enough stuff to make up for what I've discarded. The thing is, I love stuff. I love getting it and I can't bring myself to get rid of it. I'd rather go shopping than see a movie or go out drinking or read a great book.

The bigger reason, I suspect, is that most of the objects I buy and own greatly appeal to my senses. They look interesting, smell good, or are soft to the touch. I can spend a surprising amount of time experimenting with my dozens of colours of eye shadow or sniffing all of my perfumes. Does this make me weird? I also have a very short attention span with my things; I will love the fragrance of one soap today, but in a week I'll find a soap that I think smells even better. I can't imagine sticking to one signature scent for years. Either way, I don't know what to do to change, or if it's even possible. How can I learn to be happier with less?"

Next to stand up was a young man who said his name was Tom Edwards. He seemed like the joker of the meeting. He joked that we would all be calling him pig by the end of him speaking. He even made the noises. He was weird. I liked him already.

"I have an addiction to food. No, not even junk food. Just food in general. I have an addiction to takeaways and eating out. OK, so I enjoy junk food, yes, but I also enjoy trying out different salads and pastas. I like a huge variety of foods. In the last week I have spent over sixty pounds on eating out and takeaways for myself. I mean is that really bad? I would spend the same amount on food shopping if I went to Tesco's anyways. It's just saving me time and effort.

You're probably thinking "ha what a fat pig" but no that's not the case. I'm actually addicted to eating nice food that time and effort has gone into. I know that everyone enjoys eating out and ordering a takeaway once in a while. However, I know it's more than simply enjoying a meal from Nando's, or ordering a pizza from Domino's. I eat takeaway or eat out almost everyday. I can't be bothered with cooking my own food. It's just so much easier to pick up the phone and order a takeaway or drive to a restaurant and have food made for you.

I absolutely love kebabs, Nando's and pizza. I get cravings for it constantly. However, this is not a good thing. I want a career in singing and I want to lose weight. I feel that I need to cut down but I don't have the willpower to do so. This is why I am here today.

When I'm eating out or having a takeaway, I don't want it to end. My mouth waters at the thought. Eating out and getting a takeaway is different to cooking normal food at home. I like the feeling I get when I know that a lot of effort has gone into it to make it taste so good. When I'm not feeling good, I'll order myself a takeaway. It makes me feel happy inside. I know for a fact that I've spent thousands on takeaways and eating out this past couple of years.

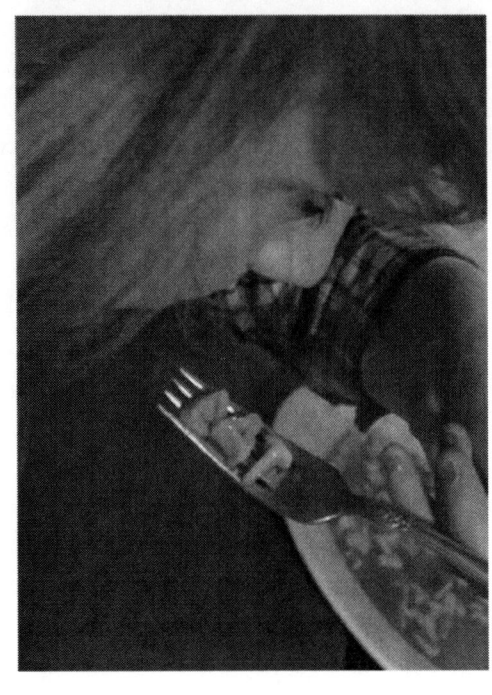

I have only ever had one bad experience when it comes to takeaways, and that was once when it made me ill, which I presume was food poisoning, but it didn't put me off. It put me off that particular restaurant but not off of that cuisine. In honestly I'm glad it made me ill, so now I have broadened my variety of places I go too for a certain food culture. That's not wrong is it?

I do like cooking, I mean I do cook, but it just doesn't taste the same. When I take the first bite of my takeaway curry my mouth just waters before my tongue even touches the spoon. I need it. I want it. But with my cooking its not the same, my tongue will touch it and it just doesn't taste right, it doesn't melt in my mouth, it makes me gag. The only cooking I would eat was my mum's but since she died, I guess I've used takeaways as my way of coping; there's no-one to cook for me, so someone else has to.

If I want to pursue a career in the entertainment business I guess I'll have to cut all this food out. It doesn't help I'm also a smoker, but if I want it that bad I will. So I've decided that I'm going to quit eating out and ordering takeaways. But it's going to take a while seeing as I had Nando's for lunch."

Everyone had a giggle. Addicted to food, who'd have thought it?

"I am addicted to shoplifting. Please don't judge me, I know it's wrong and I'm not ashamed to admit that it's wrong. I just can't help myself. Shoplifting can become an addiction because of the thrill it gives you, the same as gambling, sex or exercise would. Addiction is defined by consequences. Shoplifting has a negative impact on my life. I've been caught and I do have better things to do, yet I still do it. I'm addicted, simple.

Shoplifting is a fairly common addiction but every motivation is different. I don't shoplift because I can't afford to buy things or because I want to be stupid. I am not addicted to that at all. I am addicted to the rush I get from stealing something without being caught. The rush you get when you're a druggie is similar to the rush you get when you shoplift. You just want more and to do it all over again.

I was 14 when I first started shoplifting. Me and a bunch of friends used to hang around at the local shopping centre after school. We usually sat around with nothing to do so we'd just look around the shops having a laugh and a joke. I remember one of my friends saying that she shoplifted all the time and how easy it was. So me being me, wanted to know just how easy it was.

So a friend and I went into Boots. I knew what I was going to steal. I had wanted this new lip-gloss for ages - I had the money for it - but I didn't intend on spending it. I picked up the gloss and slide it down my school jumper. I remember walking out with fear and excitement surging through my body. I felt so proud of myself and that was it. I felt a massive high from getting away with the theft that it actually felt more rewarding that the merchandise itself. From then on I was going into shops stealing everything and anything.

I couldn't stop. I've even been caught a few times, but it's never stopped me. The rush I get is too good to stop. However, recently I was caught when I stole a dress from my favourite clothes store, and I had been followed the whole time without knowing. The security guard then chased me out of the shop and grabbed my arm, taking me back into the store. It wasn't like all the other times where they would just ask me why I did it. I was arrested. I couldn't believe it was happening to me. A permanent mark on my record, my crime will now follow me as I apply to colleges and look for jobs - not exactly what I wanted, I was also banned from the store.

That was a major wake up call and that's why I'm here today. That was a week ago and I haven't stolen since. But to be fair, I haven't even been out and about to steal anything. I know that if I go near shops I will get the urge. I need to control myself and my life. I'm thinking of applying for jobs. Just so instead of wanting to steal, I will have plenty more money to waste."

Next, a girl arrived, the colour of an orange. She was so orange that I felt like I needed sunglasses to look at her. She had bleached blonde hair and wore very skimpy clothes. She looked an absolute state. I looked around the room and saw that by the look of everyone's faces, everyone was thinking the same as me. She apologised for being late and said her name was Daisy Butler.

"I only arrived late today as I was feeding my addiction. I noticed all of you saw me when I walked in, and just to set the records straight I am not orange, it's a healthy glow. And yes, you can be addicted to tanning. Tanning is an addiction in the same way as alcoholism and a drug habit. It's my drug. Everyone's different when it comes to getting a kick. I know what I do for mine. Tanning is my thing, my love; I love to look "healthy".

Ever since I was a little girl, I always looked at other girls and wondered why they had such lovely bronzed skin. All the boys would be after them and never me. I understood why. I was unacceptably pale. So since then I always wanted to look bronzed and beautiful just like everyone else. I knew that I'd only be able to fit in with everyone else if I had a tan. So when I hit the age of fourteen, I decided enough was enough. I tried my first sun bed. Afterwards I felt so much better about myself. I actually gained some sort of confidence. I'm not being vain. It just made me feel so good.

So I've been going on a sun bed every other morning for the past 2 years. One morning I wasn't able to go and I felt immense anxiety. I dared not break the pattern of going ever again.

My mum constantly asks me the same question over and over again. What do you prefer, your looks or your life? The answer is my looks. Without my looks I have no life. That's not vanity because I accept everyone for who they are and what they look like. People just don't accept me for who I am and what I look like. My family always tells me that they prefer my natural colour and that I'm beautiful without the sun beds. They tell me that they love me for who I am and that I don't need a sun bed to look good. But that's what my family say.

Everyone else compliments me and my lovely bronzed skin. I have no problem getting attention from the boys being this colour. I had a lot of problems getting attention from boys when I was as white as a ghost. If it means getting a bit of attention, I'd rather be orange. Simple.

Not only does it make me feel good on the outside, it gives me that real emotional boost. It feels good to know that people are complimenting my bronzed skin. Some people go on holiday to relax; I go on holiday for a tan. I pay ridiculous amounts of money to go to hot countries, just so I catch the best tan. The hotter, the better. People always tell me that all the sun beds and sunbathing will come back to haunt me one day, but for now I have no side effects, so I'm not worried.

When I'm older I know that I'm going to purchase my own tanning sun bed just so it saves me time and money. I've wanted to for ages but for obvious reasons, my family won't let me. That's fine."

Other hearing her speak about her addiction to tanning, I felt sorry for her. The only reason she was tanning was to fit in. She felt that she had to be that colour for boys to like her. She believed that you have to be skinny, tanned and blonde to be accepted in life.

Next a very thin girl stood up. I suddenly became worried that she was going to snap. I felt like I needed to hold her up. It was obvious what her addiction was. I felt an instant need to help her and I didn't even know her. She was very quiet when she spoke and everyone had to sit in absolute silence to hear her. She said her name was Sophie Bumble.

"When I entered the hall this morning I made my way straight to the refreshments table, a glass of ice water and a handful of peanuts, no more, no less. I am addicted to calorie counting and dieting. I have it under control though. I just like to know what's going into my body I guess; being a 15 year old girl, I've realised this is the only thing in my life I have full control over.

I can control myself when it comes to counting the calories, but I read my magazines and all I see on the pages is images of beautiful girls, all models. Their stomachs are all so small and flat, I wish mine was like that. No-one's ever called me fat, but it's not something I need to be told, I know it already.

I mean, I didn't want to die. So like, I don't starve myself. I've got it all sorted out in my head. I make sure that I eat one piece of fruit for breakfast, a handful of nuts and a salad for lunch, and nothing for dinner. I'll only drink water too.

Food never used to be an issue to me. Mum used to feed me big portions but it was only because she wanted me to be big and strong. Its not like the food was unhealthy, but it wasn't like I was getting my five portions of fruit and vegetables. In all honesty, my mum's always been big and I've always been worried that I would end up like that.

She's always been on a diet but she never seems to stick to it, and I have never wanted to end up like that. I see pictures of my mum when she was my age and we look identical, does that mean that in 30 years time I will be the same as her? Well that's not happening. I make sure that I hardly eat anything, and when it comes to dinner time, I'll take my dinner upstairs to my bedroom and throw it straight in the bin. No-one ever questions what I'm doing, no-one really cares.

It's been like this for a year now and I know that I'm always going to be like this. No-one has and I doubt no-one ever will catch what I'm doing, it's not like I'm starving myself, I am just controlling what is going into my body. I will eat, but just the healthy stuff.

Sometimes I do treat myself and I'll eat my favorite foods like roast potatoes but I'll eat them in moderation, I don't wanna eat too many and pile on the pounds now do I? But it's not like I make myself sick, I would never do that. I wouldn't want to purposely hurt my body.

I've never had a proper boyfriend and I think that could be down to my opinion on my own body, I hate my body so much that I think everyone else will. I do want a boyfriend. I just need to build the confidence up in myself, then I'll be comfortable to have a partner.

One day this battle with food will disappear and I will finally be happy, but until then I guess it's grapes and pears for me."

Next to stand up was a girl who looked like she'd been chucked into a rainbow. She was wearing colourful clothes and had colourful hair. It's a shame she didn't seem to have a colourful personality to match. I had noticed that she hadn't smiled once throughout the meeting. She spoke with an angry tone in her voice. She said her name was Imogen Smith. "As you can see, the colour of my hair is not normal. I have bright blonde hair with random bits of pink, purple and blue. I can't even remember what my natural hair colour looks like. I'm not even joking when I say I have an addiction to dying my hair because yes, I know everyone dyes their hair once in a while, but I just can't stop. I've been dying my hair since I was eleven years old. Now I'm twenty two.

It's my hair; I can do what I like to it. I don't see a problem with it anyway. I was cooking my own dinners at the age of eight; dying my own hair is nothing. My mum thought I was mental when I first told her I was dying my hair at the age of eleven. She still tells me I am mental and has even mentioned that I should go to the doctors about my addiction. I looked at her as if she was the mental one. Why would I go to the doctors about changing my hair colour a lot?

I've had my hair just about every colour there is. I've had brown hair, black hair, red hair, blonde hair, and every hair colour of the rainbow. I'm always mixing the colours together too. I like being dramatic. My hair is like a blank piece of paper and the dye are my pens. I think of my hair as a piece of art and my way of expressing myself. Surely you can understand that?

I can never stay satisfied with one hair colour for long. Whenever I walk into a supermarket or stores like Boots, I'll head straight to the hair dye section. I'll look out for new hair colours or hair dyes to try. Sometimes I'll just buy dye for the fun of it. I know I'm obsessed with buying hair dye as I have about ten packets stacked away ready to use.

I'll dye my hair probably once every month, but it depends on certain situations. For example, when I get a boyfriend, I usually stick to the same hair colour that I had when I started going out with him. But when I break up with him, I'll completely change my hair colour. It's the same with friends, if I have an argument with a friend, I'll change my hair colour. I kinda feel like dying my hair will change my personality. It just makes me feel better and if no-one can understand that, then fine. I can do what I like with my hair. I like change. I like how different I look with different hair colours.

I hate it when people say I'm ruining my hair. "Your hair will fall out" "Your hair is so dry" "Your hair feels like straw" People ruin their life everyday with stupidity. People change their look all the time. Why aren't I allowed to change mine? Just leave me alone, I'm not ruining my life by changing my hair colour.

Dying my hair makes me feel good about myself. Admit that I've actually tried to stop dying my hair and just keep it nice and conditioned. I try and wait a few months at least. It doesn't work. I start having a mini breakdown. When I look at why I'm dying my hair in the first place, it all makes sense. The real reason is that when I'm stressed or I'm experiencing a dramatic change, I'll dye my hair. It's like my way of getting my anger out. That might seem strange but it's not to me.

People say that I dye my hair too much and I can't dislike my looks that much, but they're contradicting themselves, they say this to me with make-up on their face. I dye my hair to make myself feel better, the same way they put foundation on to make their skin look better, so what am I doing wrong. I mean, my dye is affecting the condition of my hair but it's not like it's anyone's fault but mine. OK, so I sometimes go crazy, but who doesn't? It's my hair, and I'll be the only one to suffer the consequences."

Hmmmm, I was confused. I didn't know that dying your hair could be an addiction. I didn't know you could be addicted to something so simple. There's a big difference between being addicted to something and doing something because you want to.

Next up was a disabled young boy. He said his name was Kyle Terry. He seemed to fidget a lot with his hands and wasn't really able to look anyone in the eye. He seemed sweet though, and he was praising everyone, telling them all that they were brave to come here today. Bless his heart.

"After listening to all your admiring stories of being addicted to something, I feel stupid for coming here today. When I tell you what my addiction is, please don't laugh, as I am not making it up and I am not being silly. It's not a joke when I say I am addicted to Facebook. Yes, the social networking website that allows you to update your status, post pictures, view your friends news feed, play games, etc. Yes, I bet you've all got a Facebook. I bet you go on it every now and then just to keep in contact with family and friends, maybe have a little nose around.

So when I tell people that I'm addicted, they just laugh in my face. They think that I'm being silly, but I'm not. I am truly addicted. I can't go an hour without checking it. I get scared that whilst I've been away from Facebook someone has written on my wall, status or picture. I get scared that someone new has added me and I need to accept. Recently I bought a new £35 per month mobile contract just so I can fix my addiction when I'm out and about. So even when I'm out, I am able to check my notifications. Free internet, my dream come true.

The first thing I do when I wake up is check my Facebook. The last thing I do before I go to sleep is check my Facebook. It's not like I don't have a social life or can't perform socially, because I do and I can. I attend college; I love going out and meeting new people. It's just that it's so much different socialising online. Better infact. Although I have a lot of people of whom I know and have met on my friends list, I also have many of whom I don't know and have never met. Those people don't know me and can't judge me. Yeah, OK, so they can look at my pictures. Well I look nothing like my pictures. I've tried to keep my wheelchair hidden in photos. It's not that I'm ashamed of my disability; I just don't feel the need to broadcast it over Facebook.

I've always been seen as 'different' and people have always judged me on my looks and how I act. My online friends talk to me like a 'normal' person and never in my life have I felt normal. I was badly bullied in school and I never understood why. No-one wanted to be friends with the disabled kid, so I was always alone. All I ever wanted was to be accepted for who I was. One day a really nice girl in my class spoke to me for the first time ever. She asked me if I was on Facebook, I said to her, what is Facebook? She didn't know whether I was joking or not. When she realised I was being serious, she told me all about it.

So I got myself a Facebook account about a year ago, just before my seventeenth birthday. I didn't understand it at first; it confused me - all of the different applications and such. But the more and more that I played around on it, the easier it became and I started to enjoy it. For the first time in my life I felt accepted, I felt as if I was normal. I was doing what the 'normal' people did.

I didn't really have many friends to begin with, mainly family. I didn't have anyone to add to be honest, I didn't have any friends. But gradually I added other people and slowly expanded my network. I would sometimes add people and they would comment my wall saying "Hi babe, thanks for the add, but have I ever met you?" I'd ignore and delete those type of comments, so people wouldn't think I was a weirdo. I'd then talk to these people on Facebook chat and convince them that I wasn't any stalker or strange person; I just wanted to expand my network. When I told people this they kind of realised that I was just a normal guy who just wanted a chat every now and then.

From then on I became addicted. I was comfortable sharing and connecting with others online because it wasn't as intimidating or personal as approaching someone face to face. Especially when I felt like I wasn't the same as everyone else. Sometimes people I've never met talk to me on Facebook as if they have known me forever. It's a really nice feeling.

Now whenever I get friend requests from people, I get the biggest rush of happiness ever. I just wish it could be like that in real life. No-one ever wants to be my friend. So getting a friend request online makes me feel wanted and needed. I've never had a girlfriend; no girl would ever want to be with me. I don't need a girlfriend anyway. I have online friends, who are constantly making me feel loved. I love it when my number of friends rapidly increases, it's so exciting, and if pokes on Facebook actually meant something I would have lost my virginity a long time ago. No, seriously. There's a fan page that I joined on Facebook called 'stop poking me and let's just have sex'.

My mother started complaining saying that all I ever did was go onto the computer or my phone. I was forgetting to actually socialise in the real world. I used to be very close with my mum. We'd talk about my day, her day and everything else. Now I just come home from college, grab something to eat and go straight to my room. Every time she tried talking to me, I'd almost blank her. So she had a long chat with me one night and asked me to cut back on the hours that I would usually spend on the computer. I agreed. All she wanted me to do was eat dinner at the table with the rest of the family and spend some quality family time together. However, even at the dinner table and watching television with the family, I'd go on my phone and check my notifications."

Next was a man who had the tightest t-shirt on stood up. He was gorgeous. As well as having what looked like a fantastic body with rippling muscles, he had dark chocolate eyes. I had to stop and remember where I was at. I wished I was at a speed dating meeting instead. I couldn't believe that I'd only just noticed him. He began to speak with a deep voice. He said his name was Lee, Lee Club.

"My addiction is exercising. It seems like a strange addiction, but in fact this is probably one of the most typical addictions. I don't feel ashamed of myself because it's not an addiction that can necessarily be classed as bad. It beats being addicted to partying.

I actually couldn't live without it. I go to the gym once or twice a day, that's my routine. I never miss a day and I'll go for more hours if I feel down, angry or stressed - just to pump it all out of me. I couldn't think of anywhere better to go than the gym when feeling like absolute crap. Working out at the gym makes me feel happy and focus on something else. It keeps me focused and looking forward to the days ahead. It makes me feel refreshed and ready for life's ups and downs.

I guess as well that deep down, I do go to the gym to keep in top shape. It must have something to do with wanting to look and feel good too. If I didn't go to the gym I'd feel fat, ugly and rough. Not to mention lazy and depressed. People probably think "pah, you're not addicted to the gym, you're just vain and want to look good". Well yeah, I do want to look good, but it's also so much more than that. It makes me happy, and it's the only thing that keeps me sane. When I go to the gym, I feel amazing and I see in my head that my muscles are getting bigger. I feel alive. It's most definitely an addiction as I need it on a daily basis. No-one will understand what it's like to be addicted to the gym until they go their selves. Exercise is addictive. Full stop.

To me, the gym is like breathing or eating to others; if I don't go everyday I feel weak, hopeless and empty. I go for a run every evening as well as going to the gym every morning. I'll sprint around my local park until my lungs burn and my legs feel like jelly. I always have to beat my time from the day before or I'll have to start all over. It's not a problem. I mean, I deserve to keep myself in shape right? I'm not doing any harm. One day I decided to stop and just think about my exercising. I realised that I had an exercise addiction. I have complete control of it though. Or so I thought I did.

I started reading things on the internet about exercise addictions. The internet told me everything I needed to know. In reality I didn't have any control at all. Exercise addicts go over the edge because it gives them a sense of superiority that's lacking in their life. With such a great body and their obvious discipline, other people look up to them and it gives the addict a sense of power. This statement was made for me.

I like the power and I love it when I get complimented on how big my muscles have got or how "buff" I look in my new top; it gives me a huge rush. I still don't believe that having this addiction is bad. I'm not going to stop. I'll never stop. I just wanted to come here and let everyone know that addiction can be good. I won't let anyone tell me otherwise."

"My name is Lewis Bid. Ha-ha, how typical. I bet you can just guess what my addiction is - gambling. I used to go out with fifty pound in my pocket and come home with over six hundred. I'm not a thief though, never have been, never will. It's not like my addiction is harming me, its only benefiting me. I'm a gambler and I'm in control of my addiction. I could give it up right now if someone asked me to... I think.

It only started with slot machines at arcades, it was just a bit of fun when I was on holiday and it wasn't like I was spending hundreds of pounds, it was just the odd pound here and there. Harmless fun right? I never knew that online gambling existed; I mean, I didn't even know how to work the internet. But getting a laptop was possibly one of the biggest mistakes of my life. I didn't realise that there were so many websites out there that were based on real life games. I started on some free trials and games and it just seemed like harmless fun, just something you could do for a laugh, but it got worse.

I thought a few pounds here and there would be OK, it wasn't like I was spending big bucks, a bit of late night gambling wasn't going to harm anyone. Just simple card games, it was about common sense, no mind tricks. Well, that's what I thought. Winning was so easy, I just had to think about my next move and then the money would come rolling in, simple. Gambling gave me a rush, a rush that I had never had before. I had taken drugs in the past, but no drug gave me this feeling a feeling of excitement, the feeling that could hurt me. I was a winner.

I guess every time I won money it made me want to win more as I knew I couldn't lose. But I could. I never thought of myself as a loser, I thought I was and always would be a winner, but one day I realised that my winning streak wouldn't last forever. I didn't realise how addictive online bingo would be, I mean, I wasn't addicted on real life bingo; it was just something about being online. I could play when ever I wanted, in the middle of the night was my biggest weakness, and I often couldn't sleep so I would stay up on the computer.

At first it was only a few pounds here and there, and it didn't seem to make a difference. Instead of smoking that day, I would use my fag money on playing a few games, it didn't harm my body and it made my lungs feel better, so it was the better option. Five pounds a day isn't a lot, it's a good amount, enough for a few games but not so much that my boyfriend would realise. I kept winning and winning so I decided to up the stakes a bit. I started spending more and more, OK, so I wasn't winning all the time anymore, but I was doing pretty well I guess.

I played once and lost around £750, I know it's a lot but I wasn't bothered; I thought I could win it back easily enough, but I didn't.

I tried for weeks and weeks to gain that money back, I started betting at £5 but the stake slowly rose. More and more money I was losing just so I could win this £750 back, but sadly I ended up losing more. I was so fixated on getting that money back that I didn't realise I was losing more.

I'm still trying to make that money back today, but somehow I've landed myself into more debt. One day I'll make it back, I'm sure of it. But until that day I can easily go without food, or electricity for a day, well, at least until I get my money back."

Next, two people stood up. They were quite obviously twins. I was confused. They both had an addiction? How strange.

"Hello everyone, my name's Daniel, and this is my sister Paula. We are twins, and I'm addicted to salt whereas Paula's addicted to sugar. It sounds silly that we're addicted to such nonsense. I mean, everyone loves a bit of sugar in their tea or salt on their chips, but the amount we use isn't normal. People might think we're getting confused between liking a pinch of salt or sugar here and there and being addicted to it. However, when you can't even taste the food or drink anymore and just the salt/sugar, you have a salt/sugar addiction."

Paula started to talk.

"I like 8 sugars in my tea, perfect. I like it so sweet that it overpowers the taste of the tea and it just tastes like heaven. I like anything that's sweet. I could live on cakes, chocolate or sweets, but I know that it's bad for me. I've tried to cut sugar out a lot, but I just can't; I get cravings, bad cravings. It's been like this for years. However, if you've been binging on the sugar for many years the system that processes blood sugar control fails. The pancreas produces too much insulin and therefore the level of glucose in the blood drops. It is not normal and the level of energy decreases. The person will then feel tiredness, headaches, nervous tension, and depression. Just how I feel when I go without sugar.

I binge on sweets mainly. I always get a craving for sweets in the mornings. I'll eat breakfast and leave for college, stopping off in the shop and buying packets of sweets. I will have eaten half of the sweets by the time I've got to college. Everyday I will do the same. It's not like I can avoid going into the shop because I will then get to college dying for something sweet. I'd then feel moody and want to leave college. So it's better if I just do it."

Daniel butted in.

"Ah Salt, my worst nightmare. Salt on my chips, in my sandwich and on every other food I feel that it gives my food so much more flavour, and to be honest I can't remember what food tastes like without lashings of salt. Nothing tastes nice without a pinch of salt here and there. Pasta for dinner? Not unless each bit is coated in salt. It's not silly because people get addicted to things such as caffeine all the time. This is just the same. It's a dangerous addiction. Eating too much salt can kill you. I know this addiction could potentially kill me. It's strange, because to me it's like a drug. Refusing to eat anything without salt is like refusing to go a day without smoking cannabis. When my food is not covered in salt it makes me ill and sick. I can't physically force myself to eat something that tastes bland and plain."

Next up was a strange looking woman. I'm not calling her ugly. She just looked strange. She looked quite young, but was dressed like my grandma. She stood up and smiled at everyone before introducing herself. She said her name was Charlotte Tall.

I'm addicted to television. Television addiction, you may think its harmless, but it's not, let me show you that it can be harmful to you. I came across recent research; the research proved that the number of people using drugs and the number of people who are addicted to the television programmes are the same. Some people even say that watching a lot of television is more dangerous than taking drugs. I agree.

I asked myself the following questions to know for certain whether I was addicted or not. Do I tune in only to view my favourite shows/ news? Or do I find myself channel surfing for hours on end? My answer is the second one.

You might hear of a young child or teenager being addicted to watching television. Not a 23 year old woman. A young child or teenager relies on the TV for entertainment. Most of the time kids are at home doing nothing and get into the routine of watching TV. My days and nights are spent watching television. I haven't had a job since I left college. I don't want a job. That would involve effort – something I'm not willing to give.

I like getting up in the morning, switching the telly on, and relaxing with a cup of tea. I'll switch it on in the morning and switch it off in the early hours of the next day. There's always something to watch. I have hundreds of channels. When I say that I'm addicted to television, everyone just laughs. Everyone likes a bit of television every now and then. But I know I am addicted. Addiction is essentially defined as the desire to repeat behaviour, and the inability to stop a behaviour that may have harmful consequences. I used to think I could live without it. I tried going without my TV for ONE day. Could I do it? Of course I couldn't. I realised that anyone could take my phone, my laptop, or even my bed away from me. But I would not allow you to take away my TV. If you took away my TV from me, you'd be taking away a part of me. Sounds stupid doesn't it?

Everyone has a favourite possession. Mine is my TV, end of story. I never make plans with anyone or anything if it conflicts with my favourite programmes."

The hall went quiet as it was the last person's turn to speak. She was a young girl, couldn't have been much older than me, and she looked intriguing, as if she had a story to tell.

"Hello, my name is Sarah Frank, and I am not an addict, never have, never will be. I've never drank nor smoked; it's never tempted me, I'm not here today to rub this in your face, I'm here too tell you about my baby sister Chloe. Unlike me, her mind wasn't as clear as mine. She died on the 14th of April this year due to her addiction, and she was a self harmer. A self harmer who went too far. I've never been able to admit this to anyone, not even to closest friends, but I've built up the courage to come here today and admit it. My sister was a self harmer.

I was the one who found her diary, and the entry from that chilling day. Reading it destroyed me. I never knew she felt like this, and maybe if I did I could have helped her.

March 2009

"Nothing can stop me now. I have to go. If my sister or dad ever read this then it will tell them everything they need to know.

The first time I did it I didn't even think, it just came naturally, it just felt like the pain and hurt was pouring out of me. I didn't feel like what I was doing was wrong, it only felt like it was making me feel better. The only reason I did it was because I was arguing with dad and he made me angry. People spoke about self harming before and said how it made them feel relaxed and happier, and that's what I needed.

I didn't really know what I was doing; I didn't know how to do it. I just started scratching my arms, I would push down hard and deep until my arms would go red, and when they were red I knew I was doing it right. I continued to push down until I saw my arm leak, the blood would trickle out, and at that point I felt free, I felt right for the first time in my life.

After doing it the first time it became an addiction. Any time something happened at home or someone hurt me, it was the easiest way to relieve the pain. After then it happened more and more often. I remember doing it every time dad shouted at me. Every time someone I loved and cared for hurt me emotionally, I would hurt myself.

I then slowly moved on from using my own hands, I would use anything to release the pain, keys, knifes, tweezers. I would use anything that I could push into my skin to make me release some blood. I didn't care if it wasn't clean or it wasn't safe, that didn't bother me.

I tried to disguise it all of the time, but it wasn't easy. I'm surprised no-one ever noticed. Then again, I didn't think anyone would care anyway. I'd always been a daddy's girl, you know that, but when mother left, he changed. It then became a daily thing. I thought that if I hurt myself people would stop hurting me. Dad made me feel like a bad person, and I thought if I punished myself it would make me happy. He hit me all the time, Sarah, and I thought that hurting myself would make him proud, it would make me into the person that he wanted me to be.

He didn't treat me like his little girl anymore, and I thought if I made myself look vulnerable he would love me again. It didn't work. I wanted to be his special little girl; he used to fill me with love, now he fills me with self hate. I tried my hardest to cover my shame - long sleeved t-shirts, jumpers and coats, any way to try and disguise what I truly was, a monster. I became so used to hurting myself. I mentioned it to my friends once, I asked them of their opinion on the matter, and they just laughed and turned the other way, quoting "people who are self harmers are losers trying to get attention". That really hurt me. Was I a "loser"? Did I just want attention? Well, yes. I did want attention, but only from one person, Dad. When cutting deep, I'd go through memories of Dad and I in my head. I'd look at photographs. My tears would fall so heavily. I just wanted to feel loved, and wanted.

I never thought that one day I'd feel like going this far, but then again, what is too far? The night Dad caught me made me realise. I didn't mean to get caught, all I was doing was running from the toilet to my room, I didn't realise anyone was still awake.

I heard the creaking of the floor boards behind me, and I froze. All I could see was Dad's eyes focused on my arms, and I had been caught. I thought he would see them and instantly take me into his arms and shower me with love. He didn't.

I don't remember what he said; I tried to block it out, all I could see was the anger on his face, the upset in his eyes. He told me I wasn't his little girl anymore; I was someone that he didn't know. And then I realised what had I done. How had I got myself into this state? I was a mess. I had been cutting myself for over a year, and my arms were disgusting and scarred, unattractive and sore. For the first time in my life I felt ashamed, ashamed of myself. I tried to explain everything to Dad, but the words couldn't come out. I told him I did this for him, but he didn't understand, I felt blank and empty. I could barely look him in the face and then my father did the last thing I had ever expected, he cried.

That was heartbreaking.

I'd never been in that situation before, so I didn't know what to do, how to act. He was heartbroken, and so was I. I only did this to make him happy, to make him proud, but I guess I did the complete opposite. My dad tried to build bridges in our relationship but it was hard, and it just wasn't working out. I guess the fact that I tried to impress someone made them despise me even more. I can't deal with that, and that is why I'm going to end it all."

Exactly 6 hours after this entry was dated, my father and I found her in her room, dead. Her cream carpet was stained with the colour of her own blood. Her face was pale and lifeless, I knew she was gone. I tried to run over to her, but my body was frozen, I couldn't move. I felt like I wanted to cry, but the tears didn't come.

I was heartbroken.

I feel like my soul has been ripped to pieces and I can't even look at myself with out feeling guilty now. I could have stopped her; if I had just paid more attention to her it would have all been fine. But I didn't, I feel selfish and empty. I'm not trying to shock you all, I'm only telling you this so that you know what the repercussions of your actions can be, and you don't want to end up like my beautiful little sister."

At this exact moment I felt an atmosphere in the room, I saw people sitting there speechless. This made it real for everyone, the one glistening tear on Sarah's eye showed that it was tearing her up inside, but she was being strong and I think that's what choked everyone up. To see how strong someone was, and how heartbroken she was.

They say that admitting you have a problem is the first step to battling an addiction, but I now realise its not. The first step in battling your addiction is realisation, being shocked and realising the worst that could happen if you continue with the physical or mental abuse... and it only took me one person to realise this.